Poetic Beginnings

Sanjana Arunkumar

BookLeaf Publishing

India | USA | UK

Presentation by *BookLeaf Publishing*

Web: www.bookleafpub.com

E-mail: info@bookleafpub.com

ISBN: 9789358316391

First edition 2023

ACKNOWLEDGEMENT

A special thanks go to my family and friends for helping me to write this fascinating book. It was actually very fun to write it.

I am also grateful to the countless authors, whose works have influenced and made my writing better.

Last but not least, I want to express my thanks to the readers.

Thank you for reading this book, I hope you like it!!!

PREFACE

"Poetic Beginnings" is a charming collection of verses written by a young poet. Each poem reflects the world through a child's eyes, filled with wonder, creativity, and boundless enthusiasm. These delightful poems capture the joy of storytelling, the thrill of adventure, and the whimsy of everyday life. "Poetic Beginnings" invites readers to embrace the simplicity and charm of a child's perspective. It's an exploration of life's magic through the eyes of a young poet.

Little Baby Bro

Little Baby Bro
Bring me a sparrow
That has a pretty shadow
Look in the meadow
For a little fellow
Holding a wild flower yellow
Which seems mellow
Come quickly or I'll eat your Jello !!!

Play

My goodness, what a day
It's freezing, although it's May
Mum, I'm bored I want to play
With my favourite thing - clay
All right dear, you may
But make sure you don't stay
Because we're going far away
Oh my God, I say
What's that? Tooth Decay?!
We're going to the dentist straight away !!!

Banana

There was once a Banana
Who liked to sing; Tra la la !!
Then it lost it's voice
After that a boy called Boyce
Said don't worry Banana !
With care and kindness, they'd rejoice,
Together, they found Banana's voice.

Funny Mack

The girl called Mack
Was going to pack
Her things into a box
As fast as an ox
But when she sealed it she used blue tac
With tape and boxes, she'd not relax,
Preparing for adventures in a stack.

Tricky Work

Hello, if you click
This button, I'll pick
You to show me a trick
Then draw on a stick
The shape of a brick
Then spell out prick
If you've done it, you get a tick !!

HoneyBee

There is a honeybee
That gave me honey
Near they hover
To any flower
They're quite frightening
Because they do sting
But as for me
I just leave them be !!

Volcano

I rumble and grumble
Oh, What could I be ?
From below you see
Lava leaking down me

I'm nice and mean
But blasted to the sky
Please believe me
When I say it's high !!!

Besties

There's a girl called Stacie
Who's bestie is Daisy
Stacie likes soccer
Daisy is a walker
They both like their moms
Tracy and Maisy
In their friendship, they're forever cozy,
With Stacie, Daisy, Tracy, and Maisy, it's all so
rosy!

Sunshine

The Sun rose over a bright blue sea
What a sight for everyone to see
Our body needs vitamin D, as a key
You can get that from the Sun, for free !!

Toy Shop

There was a boy who liked to hop
All the way to a nearby shop
He wanted a toy from the top
To use it as a puppet show prop
Just then his sister cried stop
The toy is actually a cop !!!

Chill in the Hill

If you want to chill
Go on the top of the hill
There you can see a windmill
It gives you such a thrill
Don't stand still
The cold weather makes you ill
Climbing uphill is a skill
Upon that hill, time stands still, a moment to
fulfill !!

Water

Oh ! Water you're so flexible

If you were in sea
You are salt water

If you were in Rain
You are Pure water

If you were in falls
You are herbal water

If you were in eyes
You are Tear

I wish humans are
Flexible like you !!

My Mummy

Mummy Mummy Mummy
You are very funny
You and I like gummy
This is very yummy
I came from your tummy
You make each day feel sunny,
Life with you is such a journey !!

Moments

Whenever we take a photo
There's always a sweet struggle to smile
Whenever the rain falls on a dry soil
There's always an earthly scent
Whenever the phone rings
There's always a brief distraction
Whenever the weather is very cold
There's always a story to be told !!!

Van

In the toy van
There's a little man
Who has a ban
To drive Campervan
But he can
Drive his four-wheeled tin can !!!

Frozen

This is the story of Frozen
You've probably watched it a dozen
But this version is true
Elsa and Anna lived in a Shoe !
Anna had a magic power
And Elsa had a friend in an abandoned tower !!

Boy of Troy

Hello Young Boy!
Are you in Troy?
Is it destroyed?
Or is it full of joy?
Did you enjoy?
Or did you get annoyed?
You didn't bring your toy
Then of course you are annoyed
Believe me, silly boy
Next time bring a toy !!

Beach

I love the beach
It's as pretty as a peach
And if you're lucky
But not unlucky
Your teacher might go there to teach !!

Bear

This is a story of Bear
The bear had long hair
And she was as fast as a hare
You could meet her if you dare
But then you'd be quite shy
And her house was very high !
If you pass by
She'll give you a Pie !!

Earth

We live in Earth
In it, there's South, East, West and North
It gave birth
To us, so it's worth
With every day's rebirth,
In nature's arms, we find our true worth !!

New Year

O pretty mirror dear
You show my face clear
When I stand near
All the fairies cheer
Earth is a sphere
Don't you fear
All the fun is here
It's a New Year !!!